JB Bie
Bernard, Jan, author.
Justin Bieber

# Justin Bieber

BY JAN BERNARD

Published by The Child's World®
1980 Lookout Drive • Mankato, MN 56003-1705
800-599-READ • www.childsworld.com

Acknowledgments
The Child's World®: Mary Berendes, Publishing Director
The Design Lab: Cover and interior design
Amnet: Cover and interior production
Red Line Editorial: Editorial direction

Photo credits
Helga Esteb/Shutterstock Images, cover, 1; Featureflash/
Shutterstock Images, 5, 19, 23; Left Eyed Photography/
Shutterstock Images, 7; Phelan M. Ebenhack/AP Images for Best
Buy, 9; Seth Poppel/Yearbook Library, 11; Irving Shuter/Getty
Images, 13; PressureUA/Shutterstock Images, 14; Music4mix/
Shutterstock Images, 17; Sean Pavone Photo/Shutterstock
Images, 21; Evan Agostini/AP Images, 25; Larry Busacca/WireImage
for Turner/Getty Images, 27; Joe Seer/Shutterstock Images, 29

Design elements
Sergey Shvedov/iStockphoto

ISBN 9781614732914
LCCN 2012933680

Printed in the United States of America
Mankato, MN
July 2012
PA02128

# Table of Contents

# CHAPTER 1

# Who Would Have Guessed It?

Who would have thought that a YouTube video could make such an impact? It did for Justin Bieber. A short video posted to the Web site helped Justin rise to the top of pop music. Justin could hardly believe it himself. In fact, his dream was to become a star hockey player. Music turned out to be Justin's calling, though. He became the first solo artist to have three number-one albums before turning 18.

Justin grew up playing hockey in his small hometown in Canada. Now he tours the world playing to millions of fans. It was an amazing rise to fame. Even more amazing was that it all started before his 14th birthday!

**Justin performs in Los Angeles, California, in 2010.**

# CHAPTER 2

# An All-Canadian Boy

Justin Drew Bieber was born on March 1, 1994, in Stratford, Ontario. His mom and dad separated when he was only ten months old. His dad, Jeremy, took jobs in other cities. That meant Justin did not see his dad very often. Justin lived mostly with his mom, Pattie. They lived in public housing. The government helps pay the rent in public housing.

Pattie worked any job she could get while Justin stayed in day care. Sometimes he stayed with

Justin wrote the song "Down to Earth" about his parents' separation.

**Justin's mom Pattie supported Justin's musical talents when he was growing up.**

his grandparents. But he never felt poor because he had lots of love from his mom, grandparents, and other family members.

# CHAPTER 3

# A Musician's Beginnings

Most people know Justin as a singer. He is much more musical than that, though. Justin's first musical love was drumming. Even as a toddler, he loved to keep the beat. Pattie liked to play pop music on her stereo. So Justin banged along on pots and pans and anything else he could find.

Justin began truly learning to play drums when he was four. A **praise band** played music at Justin's church.

Justin went to an elementary Catholic French immersion school. That means most subjects were taught in French. That helps kids learn the language faster.

**Justin's first musical love was playing the drums.**

The drummer for that band taught Justin to play a real drum set. It was not long before Justin's playing started to sound like real music. Justin's mom could not afford a drum set for him, though. So a member of their church raised money to buy one for Justin.

# CHAPTER 4

# Growing Up

Pattie could not afford formal music lessons for Justin. But Justin knew how he wanted his drums to sound. So he decided to learn to get better on his own. Justin was not limited to drums. His dad Jeremy had played guitar. Jeremy and his friends gave Justin one of their old ones. Jeremy also introduced Justin to rock music. They would listen to bands such as Aerosmith, Bob Dylan, and Metallica. Jeremy even helped Justin learn to play some of those rock songs on guitar.

Justin had some informal music lessons. However, he largely taught himself to play the trumpet, guitar, piano, and drums. He hopes to learn how to play the violin, too.

**Justin in eighth grade**

Justin was a solid student. But he was always a class clown. He loved to play pranks on people. That sometimes got him in trouble. In middle school, a teacher once sent Justin to the principal's office for clowning around in class. Justin walked to the principal's office. But he did not go in. Instead, Justin walked right out the door and to his grandparents' house. His grandparents were not impressed. Justin's grandpa took him right back to school. Then Pattie grounded him!

# CHAPTER 5

# YouTube Sparks a Star

Justin decided to take his music public at age 12.
He entered a local talent show for kids ages 12 to 18.

**Justin performs on a street in his hometown in Canada.**

**Justin used YouTube and other social media sites to gain fame.**

Justin did not win. But he enjoyed singing in front of people. After that, Justin started **busking**. That means singing on the street for money. Justin was so popular that in only two hours he earned $200!

Justin's mom had recorded a video of Justin's talent show performance. Then she put it on YouTube for the rest of their family to see. She was not the only one to post videos of Justin, though. Some other people had posted videos of Justin busking. Justin and his mom noticed 100 people had watched his videos. Then that number grew to 1,000. One video got 72,000 hits. Something was going on!

# CHAPTER 6

# Something Special

Music fans were not the only people watching Justin's videos. An **agent** named Scott "Scooter" Braun watched them as well. Braun was so impressed that he called Justin's school to get Justin's phone number. The school instead gave Braun's number to Justin's mom. However, she did not trust people in the music industry. Pattie decided not to call back. Braun worked hard to get Pattie's attention, though. She finally agreed to see him. "I see something really special in your son," he told her.

Life began moving quickly after posting that first YouTube video. Seven months later, Justin and Pattie flew to Atlanta, Georgia, to meet with Braun.

**Justin poses with his manager, Scott "Scooter" Braun.**

He became Justin's **manager**. The group decided Justin would keep making videos for YouTube. That would help build his fan base. Creating an album would come later.

In early 2008, Braun told Justin to make a video singing "With You" to post on YouTube. Justin had just gotten a bad haircut. But Pattie made the video anyway. Justin had a poster of Bart Simpson on his wall. He said he thought his hair looked just like Bart's. In fact, the haircut was so bad that Braun told Justin to take the video off YouTube and record a new one. But something stopped them. The video already had 25,000 hits! So they decided to leave it posted. Many more people watched it after that.

# CHAPTER 7

# It All Begins

In early 2008, Braun called Justin with some exciting news. Famous musicians Usher and Justin

**Usher became like a brother to Justin and helped Justin with his music.**

Timberlake had watched his video. Now both wanted to work with Justin. Again, Justin and Pattie headed to Atlanta. Justin was still two weeks shy of his 14th birthday when he met with the artists. He decided to work with Usher.

Usher has since become one of Justin's **producers** and a good friend. "[Usher is] like a big brother to me," Justin said. "We just hang out and don't really talk about music a lot. We go go-karting and to arcades and movies."

Usher helped Justin get a record deal with Island Def Jam. That is a very important recording company. Usher could see that Justin was about to get very famous, very fast. So the older singer gave Justin advice. Usher told Justin

Justin hates elevators, especially when they are crowded. He said he loves video games, the Toronto Maple Leafs hockey team, and girls.

Justin and his mom moved to Atlanta, Georgia, to start his professional music career.

to be careful about how he spent his money. He also told Justin to stay humble.

Justin and his mom decided it was time to move to a bigger city. So they sold everything except their clothes and his guitar and moved to Atlanta. Justin got a tutor there. He would be working too much to go to a regular school. He also started working with Usher's voice coach.

# CHAPTER 8

# Rise to Fame

Justin's first single was "One Time." The only **publicity** for the song came from Justin's Facebook and Twitter accounts. Yet it rose to number two on

**Justin performs at a concert in England.**

the online music store iTunes. He then released three more songs that also did very well on the online music store. Braun and Usher helped Justin put together songs for his first two albums. They were to be called *My World* and *My World 2.0*. Justin's first album came out in March 2010. By then, he already had four singles that were huge hits. All four songs had ranked in the top 40 before the album came out. That had never happened to any artist before.

Justin began his first concert tour after his second album was released. He performed in 85 cities within six months.

Justin's mom goes with him on all of his concert tours. It takes more than 500 people, 18 buses, and many 18-wheel trucks to take his show on the road.

# CHAPTER 9

# Stardom

Justin opened for country singer Taylor Swift in 2009. Approximately 12,000 people watched the performance. But it was one Justin would soon want

**Even a broken foot could not stop Justin from performing.**

to forget. He hit a dip in the floor during his first song. It resulted in a broken foot! Justin finished the song, hobbled offstage, and cried. He had to get a huge boot-like cast. He could not skateboard, or do much of anything, for eight weeks. Justin could keep performing, though, as long as he was careful.

He was invited to perform for President Barack Obama for *Christmas in Washington* in 2009. One thing he did not want to do was go onstage in that boot. So Justin went against orders and performed with his boot off. Justin also performed at *Christmas in Washington* in 2011.

Justin has won many awards. Among them was the American Music Awards' 2010 Artist of the Year. He was also a big hit in the 2011 Nickelodeon Kids' Choice Awards. Justin won the Favorite Song and Favorite Male Singer awards there. The Favorite Song award was for the song "Baby." Justin helped cowrite the song. Justin's album *My World 2.0* also won Top Pop Album of 2011 at the Billboard Music Awards.

**Justin meets with President Barack Obama at *Christmas in Washington* in 2011.**

# CHAPTER 10

# A New Life

Justin has made a lot of money as a music star.
But he has worked hard to follow Usher's advice.
Justin often shares his money and time with others.
He supports several **charities**.
Among them are the
Make-a-Wish Foundation
and the Children's Wish
Foundation. Both
organizations grant
wishes to sick children.
Justin has given both his
money and his time to help
sick kids. Justin has also given
money to food banks. He remembers a time growing
up when he and his mom relied on food banks to eat.

**One of the most popular wishes through the Make-a-Wish Foundation is to meet a celebrity. Meeting Justin was a very popular wish in 2010.**

**Justin smiles for the cameras at the 2011 American Music Awards.**

Justin is at the beginning of what looks to be a long career. With the help of his mom, grandparents, and Usher, he has remained humble. As Justin said, "The success I've achieved comes to me from God, through the people who love and support me, and I include my fans in that."

# GLOSSARY

**agent (AY-juhnt):** An agent manages the business side of an entertainer's career. Scott "Scooter" Braun is an agent.

**busking (BUHSK-ing):** Busking is performing in public with the hope people will give you money. Justin became famous for his busking.

**charities (CHAR-i-tees):** Charities are organizations that provide money or assistance to those in need. Justin gives his time and money to several charities.

**manager (MAN-i-jur):** A manager organizes an entertainer's daily life. Scott "Scooter" Braun is Justin's manager.

**praise band (PRAZE band):** A praise band plays a modern type of music used in Christian church services. Justin listened to a praise band at church.

**producers (pruh-DOOS-urs):** Producers find the money to make an album and supervise its production. Usher is one of Justin's producers.

**publicity (puh-BLIS-i-tee):** Publicity is interest or attention. Social media Web sites created publicity for Justin's music.

# FURTHER INFORMATION

## BOOKS

Bieber, Justin. *First Step 2 Forever: (100% Official)*. New York: Bieber Time Books, 2010.

Parvis, Sarah. *Justin Bieber*. Kansas City, MO: Downtown Books Inc., 2010.

Scholastic. *Justin Bieber Quiz Book*. New York: Scholastic, 2011.

## WEB SITES

Visit our Web site for links about Justin Bieber: **childsworld.com/links**

*Note to Parents, Teachers, and Librarians: We routinely verify our Web links to make sure they are safe and active sites. So encourage your readers to check them out!*

# INDEX

# ABOUT THE AUTHOR

Jan Bernard has been an elementary teacher in both Ohio and in Georgia, and has written curriculum for schools for over seven years. She also is the author of seven books. She lives in West Jefferson, Ohio, with her husband and their dog, Nigel. She has two sons.